A Short History
of
North Platte

*When Our Town Grew
and When It Didn't*

and

The Reform Election
Of 1951

along with

*Some Interesting Dates
from
1866 through 2003*

By
Keith Blackledge

A publication of the Lincoln County
Historical Society with the help of a gift
from James and Rhonda Seacrest

From Mom 8/05

North Platte, Nebraska 69101

Printed in the United States of America
by The Covington Group - Kansas City, Missouri

Published by
the Lincoln County Historical Society

Cover Design by Patsy Smith
Interior Book Design/Layout
by Alice Mora - Traveler Marketing and Publishing
www.nptraveler.com

Library of Congress number: 2005929096

A Short History of North Platte by Keith Blackledge

p. cm

Summary: *When North Platte grew and when it didn't, and the pivotal reform campaign of 1951.*

ISBN 0-9763676-0-2

Introduction

There is much about our town that isn't told in this slim volume. But it provides an overview of the good times and not so good times that says something about how towns grow and why local leadership is important.

It is also intended to give today's readers a picture of the 1951 city election and its aftermath. I believe this was a pivotal event in the town's history that deserves to be documented in some detail, reminding us that citizen action can bring about change.

There are many other gaps still not filled in what is written and thus preserved about the past of an unusually interesting town. The exploits of William F. "Buffalo Bill" Cody, have been told over and over. Pioneers Ira Bare and Bill McDonald put together *An Illustrated History of Lincoln County* which tells about what went on from 1866 to 1920. But after 1920 much of our town's history exists only in the microfilmed pages of old newspapers.

There are notable exceptions. Nellie Snyder Yost's novel, *Evil Obsession*, about Annie Cook and the county poor farm tells a grim piece of our history. Bob Greene's *Once Upon A Town: The Miracle of the North Platte Canteen* memorializes a bright spot well worth remembering. But the less dramatic stories also deserve a telling.

Like most towns, we are subject to periods when all seems negative and downhill, and other periods when optimism is boundless. A look at when our town grew and when it didn't suggests that things are never as hopeless as they seem during the worst times, and even the best times have a down side.

A lifetime of watching, reporting and commenting as a reporter and editor convinces me every town grows on the shoulders of citizens and leaders who remain positive in good times or bad. That message bears repeating as the town and the world move into the 21st Century.

Patsy Smith contributed the cover art. Alice Mora at Traveler Marketing and Publishing (www.nptraveler.com) did the layout. Jim and Rhonda Seacrest, former North Platte residents now living in Lincoln, provided financial support to make publication possible.

My thanks to the North Platte Public Library, the Lincoln County Historical Society, and the North Platte Telegraph for the resources that make much of this information available. Thanks also to many readers who have offered comments, suggestions and ideas over the years. Your questions have led me to believe there is an interest in the history of our town. And thanks to my wife, Mary Ann, whose help in checking my copy, dealing with publication details and in many other ways is invaluable.

Readers will no doubt find some errors and many omissions. You are invited to call them to my attention by writing to me at 1214 West E, North Platte, or at keithbma@charter.net. God willing, I hope to write a more detailed history of North Platte in the 20th Century.

Table of Contents

Book One

Short History of One Town:

Leadership makes a difference

When we grew and when we didn't: Remembering some town builders

Seek the welfare of the city where I have sent you .... for in its welfare you will find your welfare. - Jeremiah 29:7

That is good advice. We are citizens of a state and nation and of a larger world. But we do most of our living in the city we were sent to, or at least where we live right now. Most of us can do little to change the course of national or international events. But we can all do something to make the place we live better.

I have a fondness for town builders, the individuals who go out of their way to make their town better. There are some in every town, in every era. Sometimes their projects succeed, sometimes they don't. But the effect generally is one of moving forward.

Looking at our town's history, I was struck by how much is revealed in the census figures, decade by decade. Mostly we've moved ahead. Some of it was our own doing, some of it, especially the "down" periods, seemed determined mostly by economic or natural events beyond our control.

There has been much controversy in recent years about whether we should offer incentives to help our town grow. We've always done it. Spending money to attract new investment and jobs has been a part of our town's history from the beginning. I suspect it is part of the history of every town that survives.

Here as examples are a couple of stories from old North Platte newspapers. One called *The Independent Era* printed this item in its July 30, 1903 edition.

Our local committee that went to Lincoln Monday to present North Platte's claim for the permanent state normal school, returned Wednesday.

They found fourteen competitors for the school, some of them with "stunning" propositions in the way of bonuses to the state in return for the school. For instance, the city of Hastings offers what figures out to be equal to a cash bonus of $131,000....

Kearney, Broken Bow and Ord are thought to be our strongest competitors on account of geographical location, but our committee seems to think that North Platte is still in the list of probabilities. Our offer aggregates $20,000, including the site.

The school went to Kearney. If it had happened differently, our town would be different today and so would Kearney.

We did get something in 1903, and at the time it may have seemed a bigger prize than the state normal school. This story appeared in *The Independent Era* in August that year.

At a meeting of the citizens last night at the court house a finance committee of eleven members, with H. S. White as chairman, was appointed whose duty it also will be to receive bids, determine on several suitable propositions as sites for the farm, raise such subscription of cash as is deemed necessary and work with the University committee for the location of the farm.

The committee included W. W. Birge, John Bratt and W. H. McDonald, among names some might recognize today. The "state farm" opened in 1904. It is known today as the University of Nebraska West Central Research and Extension Center. Half the money for the original land purchase was donated by local citizens. Then, as now, you seldom get something without some local investment.

I've looked with some envy at what the "normal school," now the University of Nebraska at Kearney has meant to that city. But I'm also grateful to the leaders in our town who worked and raised money to bring the experiment station here. If it had gone elsewhere, we would have missed out on Glenn Viehmeyer's mums, Dale Lindgren's penstemons, Gail Wicks's softball teams and much more.

In every time there are decisions and actions that shape a town's future. And always those decisions and actions depend on leaders with vision and energy and a desire to make a difference. They also depend on leaders willing to take risks and make investments for the long term. And they cannot succeed without some measure of public support and trust. Sometimes we have those things, sometimes we don't.

There are many leaders who made a difference in our town's history. My list would include Mendel Hirschfeld, who raised the funds to make Scout's Rest Ranch a State Historical Park, and

M e n d e l Hirschfeld was chairman of a 1960-61 campaign to raise $37,500, half the cost of buying Scout's Rest Ranch for use as a state historical park. The state promised to come up with the other half. There were complaints about the purchase price and the drive took nearly a year. Hirschfeld later was president of the first board of Mid-Plains Vocational-Technical School when it survived intense opposition, lawsuits, and an area-wide election that might have killed it. He served on that board until his death in 1981.

Brown-Harano Studio

who also headed the Mid-Plains Vocational Technical School board in its difficult beginnings when a lesser man might have bailed out. A history of the 20th century in our town would recognize the leadership of Wendell Wood in finding ways to keep that school alive, and even more in building a new hospital that launched a new era in health care for our town.

Telling those stories will require a larger book. Meanwhile, the broad brush strokes of population figures tell quite a story in themselves.

There was no town here until the railroad came in 1866, and not much after the construction crews moved on in 1867. Things moved slowly at first. A town charter was drawn up in September, 1873, but we didn't really get a city government until 1875. The "Panic of 1873" brought on a national depression that lasted through 1878. Our population was listed as 363 in 1880.

The Post Office and Federal Building at Fifth and Jeffers was completed in 1913. It housed the first classes of North Platte Junior College in 1965 and became Mid-Plains Community College area office headquarters in 1981. It was purchased by businessman Al Erickson in 2000 and donated to the city in 2001.

Then things started happening. By 1890, North Platte had grown to 3,055 Imagine what an exciting time that must have been! If you ran a store (or a saloon); if you were a carpenter or a banker or a lawyer, there was plenty of business. If you were a town builder, anything seemed possible.

Then the town hit a wall. There was almost no growth between 1890 and 1900. The first five years of that decade were marked by severe drought. A national depression brought on by the Panic of 1893 slowed business everywhere. From a feeling of unbounded optimism about the town's future in the 1880s, there must have been serious doubts during the 1890s.

In the new century, the town took off again. It grew by 31 percent between 1900 and 1910, to 4,793. Then it more than doubled in size between 1910 and 1920, when it hit 10,466. That's more than 5,000 new residents in10 years. Some folks who thought the town was about to die in the 1890s probably worried about it getting too large in the early 1900s.

Lots of things were happening and we can still see traces of some of them. A newspaper story in 1908 celebrated the efforts of Congressman Moses P. Kinkaid who had "engineered through congress" funds of $110,000 for a federal building in North Platte. It was our post office until 1964, then became our junior college in 1965, and the area community college headquarters until 2000. A plan to give it still another life as city offices and community rooms is on the table, but under attack, for decision in the first decade of the 21st century.

<table>
<tr><th colspan="1" align="center">North Platte Population:</th></tr>
</table>

North Platte Population:
1870-not counted
1880-363
1890 - 3,055
1900 - 3,640
1910 - 4,793
1920 - 10,466
1930 - 12,061
1940 - 12,429
1950 - 15,433
1960 - 17,184
1970 -19,477
1980 - 24,509
1990 - 22,605
2000 - 23,878

The Keith Theater opened in 1908, the Carnegie Library in 1912, the Post Office and Federal Building in 1913. The newspaper described a "massive brick building, two stories in height," completed on Front Street in 1918 for a fire station and city offices. (In more recent years, it was abandoned by the city, condemned and scheduled for demolition before it was renovated for apartments and offices by Larry Steele.)

There must have been a feeling that the future was unlimited. In one year, 1917, voters approved separate bond issues to finish the new Franklin Junior High, build that first City Fire Station, and build a new South River bridge.

The Chamber of Commerce organized private funding to buy land and build an airport in 1921.

Growth continued during the 1920s, so that North Platte was just over 12,000 population in the 1930 census, a 15 percent increase. There had been three decades of strong growth. Surely those were good years to be living here, good years to be building a business or working to build a community.

As the "Roaring Twenties" drew to a close, we were building a new high school and a new hospital. Joe Hirschfeld had started the successful effort to raise funds for the hospital. Then the depression hit and the building stood an empty shell because people couldn't pay their pledges.

Hirschfeld and others didn't give up. Keith Neville was chairman of the group that found a religious order to finish and run St. Mary Hospital, so that it could finally open in 1934. Most people think of Neville as the young man who went to

Lincoln as the "Boy Governor" during World War I. But he came home after that one term as governor and played an important role in many town-building enterprises during the 1920s. He was a major figure later in the fight for the power and irrigation development so important to the economy of the entire region today.

Even in the depression years, our town was putting infrastructure in place that would fuel growth in decades to come. In 1935, a dinner at the Pawnee Hotel marked the opening of the last link to be paved on Highway 30, the Lincoln Highway. It was the nation's first hard-surfaced road running from coast to coast and the beginning of North Platte's thriving auto tourism industry. The Jeffers Viaduct carrying that rapidly increasing traffic over the railroad opened in 1937.

But we grew by only 238 in the 30s, and the depression bred a cautious attitude in many civic leaders and institutions that sometimes hampered development later.

Growth began again in the 1940s. Wartime rail traffic was a factor. Native son Bill Jeffers had become president of the Union Pacific in 1937, when we celebrated his rise from call boy to president with a dinner seating 850 at Jeffers Pavilion.

Joe Hirschfeld was president of the Chamber of Commerce when he pushed for development of a community hospital and then headed a successful fund drive for its construction in 1929. When the onset of the Great Depression meant some donors could not make good on their pledges, the new building remained an empty shell. Hirschfeld and others stuck with the project and finally found a Catholic order willing to complete the hospital. It became St. Mary Hospital, and is now the Craft State Office Building.

Brown-Harano Studio

A young woman named Rae Wilson volunteered to organize a canteen to provide a welcome to military personnel from trains stopping at North Platte, and asked Jeffers for permission to use part of the Union Pacific Depot. Our town gained a place in World War II history that would last well into the next century. Volunteers from North Platte and 124 surrounding communities served six million service men and women between 1941 and 1946. The Canteen was

Keith Neville was elected governor of Nebraska as a Democrat in 1916. He ran for a U.S. Senate seat in 1918 and was defeated. As a civic and business leader in North Platte during the boom days of the 1920s, he made a lasting mark with construction of the Hotel Pawnee, Fox Theater and others. He headed efforts that brought the Sisters of St. Francis to North Platte in 1934 to finish and operate St. Mary Hospital. He was a major figure in the campaign for the "Sutherland Project," for irrigation and power generation during the 1930s.

Courtesy Irene Neville Bystrom

remembered in hundreds of letters, magazine articles, television programs and in 2002 in a book by Bob Greene called *"Once Upon A Town: The Miracle of the North Platte Canteen."* That generated a new round of attention, including a Nebraska Educational Television documentary. *"The Canteen Spirit,"* in 2004.

By the time Jeffers retired in 1946 the plans were forming for construction of the railroad's first hump yard here in 1948. Our population grew by 3,004, more than 24 percent between 1940 and 1950.

The city election of 1951 was one of the major turning points in our history. Publicity about high school boys frequenting the houses of prostitution helped generate support for a group determined to elect a city administration that would end

Wendell Wood and Bob Phares cut the plaster "cast" opening of the Great Plains Regional Medical Center in 1975. Wood was (as James Denny described him in an Omaha World-Herald article) "The glue that held it together" during a controversial effort from 1969 to 1975 for the purchase two aging hospitals and their merger into a single, modern facility. Phares was the mayor who initiated the study leading to the project. It was a critical turning point for health care and economic growth for the city.

Great Plains Regional Medical Center

open prostitution and gambling for which the town had long been infamous.

Chris Rosenberg was one of several community leaders who met in early 1951 to tackle that problem. He suggested Kirk Mendenhall as a candidate for mayor because he had the strength and integrity to get the job done and was in a business that couldn't be damaged by local reaction. In April the Citizens Committee slate of Mendenhall for mayor, Ed Johannesen, Bill Heming, Dale Keeney and Vern Lyons for city council, won by a landslide in the biggest turnout in North Platte voting history up to that time.

There had been cleanup campaigns before. This one stuck even though the reform mayor was booted out in the next election. I've always believed that much of the progress during the next 50 years could not have happened until that one issue had finally been put to rest.

Our town experienced no growth in the 1890s, then three decades of vigorous growth. We hit nearly a dead stop in population growth during the 1930s. From 1940 on there were four decades of strong growth before another slow-down in the 1980s.

The 1960s were landmark building years. The Chamber of Commerce and the Historical Society raised half the funds to buy Scout's Rest Ranch and make it a state historical park. The Junior College opened in 1965 and the Vocational-Technical School in 1968. Interstate 80 was completed to North Platte in 1966. Nebraskaland Days came to our town in 1968. That was the same year the eastbound hump, the new Bailey Yard, was completed.

The momentum continued through the 1970s.

The $10 million Union Pacific Diesel Repair Shop opened in 1971. Construction began on the $4 million Mall Shopping Center that year. The State built the grandstand for the Wild West Arena in 1972.

Those were bonuses from outside sources. But local leadership brought about two major initiatives in the 1970s. They were improvements important to future growth, and they came about only after intense controversy. Great Plains Regional Medical Center was dedicated in 1975, climaxing an effort that began when Mayor Robert Phares asked businessman Wendell Wood to chair a hospital study committee in 1969. In spite of intense opposition from a vocal minority, Wood succeeded in negotiating purchase of the two existing hospitals and construction of a modern new facility. A successful $1.2 million campaign for private donations, by far the largest in North Platte's history, made that possible.

Also in 1975, voters approved a $10 million bond issue to build a new junior high, a new elementary school, and improvements at six elementary schools.

It was a time again when anything seemed possible. While the schools and hospital were being built, we also voted bonds for a City Recreation Center, which opened in April, 1976.

Janet McDonald's 1972 bequest of $1 million to the North Platte Board of Education for a Junior College build-

The Fox Theater, just east across Bailey Street from the Hotel Pawnee, was built by Keith Neville and Alex Beck, also the builders of the hotel. The theater's grand opening was Nov. 24, 1929. It is also listed on the National Register of Historic Places. The theater was donated to the North Platte Community Playhouse by the four daughters of Keith and Mary Virginia Neville in 1980, and was renovated by the Playhouse as the Neville Center for the Performing Arts.

Photo by M.A.Mora - www.nebraskavisions.com

---

ing launched the Mid-Plains Community College McDonald-Belton campus. Another $10,000 in her will prompted the start of the long delayed Lincoln County Historical Museum, dedicated as a local landmark during the nation's bicentennial celebration in 1976.

The economy was stimulated by as many as 2,000 construction workers while the Gerald Gentleman coal-fired power station was built at Sutherland. Consolidated Freightways had located 300 families at a division point here. Work was going on at the new $40 million westbound hump yard, dedicated in July, 1980.

In the 1980 census we hit 24,509 and jumped from seventh to the fourth largest city in the state, behind Omaha, Lincoln and Grand Island.

Then the major construction projects were finished. Consolidated Freightways left. There was a major national recession, made worse in this area by bad times for agriculture.

So between 1980 and 1990, we lost population, shrinking from more than 24,000 to 22,605, a 1,904 drop, the largest of any city in the state.

There was a good deal of negative talk in those years. Comments like "Last one to leave turn out the lights," appeared in letters to the editor and on talk radio. Still, things were happening. Construction began on the Willow Street Viaduct in 1981 and it was dedicated in November, 1982. The next spring, the Jeffers Viaduct was closed for widening and other improvements. It reopened in August, 1984.

In the middle of a recession, a committee chaired by Jim Seacrest raised $265,000 in donations to renovate the Neville Center for the Performing Arts after the old Fox Theater building was donated to the Community Playhouse by the four daughters of Keith Neville. The grand opening was held on Dec. 9, 1983. The Buffalo Bill viaduct opened in 1989.

By 1990, things were on the upswing again. From 1990 to 2000 we got back much of what we had lost in the 1980s, growing 1,273 to 23,878.

Much of the new energy came from expansion of the medical community made possible by the decision to build a new hospital some 20 years earlier. A $7.57 million expansion project began at Great Plains Regional Medical Center in 1990, helped by a $1.3 million fund campaign. Construction began in 1994 on a privately funded $3.1 million Physicians Office Building north of the hospital. In 1996, Bill and Joan Callahan gave property valued at nearly $2 million to develop the Cancer Center later named for them.

The Flying J Travel Plaza opened in 1997. Renovation of the Camino Inn, the former Holiday Inn, began after a group of new owners headed by Pat Keenan took it over in 1998. It became the Quality Inn and Suites and Sandhills Convention Center, a major improvement in North Platte's ability to attract state and regional meetings. An addition to the North Platte Senior Center was completed in 1998, and the Boys and Girls Home of Nebraska moved into its new building.

The new century has all the earmarks of being as busy and exciting for our town as was the beginning of the previous century. Another hospital addition has been completed, a $23 million project. The new high school opened in

2003. The Wal-Mart Distribution Center and its 600 new jobs made growing pains and growing opportunities. The East Bypass was completed and a new Community Day Care Center opened.

Is "history" worth while? PBS News Hour anchor Jim Lehrer is quoted in the July/August 2004 issue of *Preservation* magazine:

"All of us should always try to see today through the prism of yesterday. We are who we are because of what others who came before us thought and did. To have only contemporary values is to have no values."

We all sense that, although we don't often put it in words. It is as true for a small town as for a state or nation. What our town is today is built upon what someone else did or thought or didn't do along the time line that is called "history."

We are part of that continuing process. Looking back once in a while gives us a perspective on where we are, and what we might become.

Landmarks Along The Way
Some selected dates in North Platte and Lincoln County history

1866 — Lincoln County organized from part of what had originally been designated as "Shorter County." First meeting of county commissioners held Oct. 1 at Cottonwood Springs.

1866 — Gen. Grenville M. Dodge of the Union Pacific lays out town site for North Platte.

November, 1866 — Union Pacific track completed to North Platte.

Jan. 31, 1867 — North Platte town site plat filed with Clerk of the Court.

June, 1867 — Terminus of railroad moved to Julesburg, Colo. North Platte drops from about 2,000 people to a few hundred. North Platte designated a division point on the railroad beginning a new period of more permanent growth.

Oct. 8, 1867 — Twenty-one votes cast in election moving county seat from Cottonwood Springs to North Platte.

Spring, 1868 — Rumor of pending Indian attack sends women and children to refuge in the roundhouse. Attack never materializes.

1868 — School District 1 organized. Classes begin with eight students in a log structure at what is now Fifth and Dewey. It was built through private donations.

Sept. 24, 1868 — Indian leaders called to "peace council" held in new Union Pacific shops at North Platte, with General William Tecumseh Sherman leading the government delegation.

May 10, 1869 — Golden spike driven at Promontory Point, Utah, celebrating completion of the transcontinental railroad.

Jan. 12, 1872 — Grand Duke Alexis of Russia arrives in North Platte by train for buffalo hunt guided by William F. Cody in Hayes County.

Sept. 13, 1873 — North Platte incorporated as a town by action of the County Commissioners. Five town trustees were appointed.

1873 — New school house erected to replace log school. Cost: $16,000.

June 13, 1873 — North Platte Cemetery Association formed, purchasing five acres at $20 an acre.

1874 — Weather Bureau records begin for North Platte.

Nov. 26, 1875 — Ordinance incorporating North Platte as a city of the second class read at a meeting of the trustees and adopted a week later.

Dec. 18, 1875 — Anthony Ries, 30, foreman of the car department with the Union Pacific Railroad, elected North Platte's first mayor, defeating C. L. Cooper, 53, a livery stable operator and former mayor of Plattsmouth. Ries won 137 to 98.

Dec. 28, 1875 — First City Council meeting.

Jan. 1, 1878 — Charles McDonald moves the iron safe and accounts he had purchased from the Walker brothers to his store and establishes the Banking House of Charles McDonald, later the McDonald State Bank, eventually United Nebraska Bank, then TierOne Bank.

May 6, 1879 — Council votes North Platte the first "dry" town in Nebraska. Saloonkeepers call booze "buttermilk" and keep on selling.

April 14, 1881 — North Platte Telegraph founded as a weekly newspaper by James McNulty.

July 4, 1882 — Col. William F. Cody stages "Old Glory Blowout" as town's Independence Day celebration at area that is now the lake in Cody Park. This was the inspiration for Buffalo Bill's Wild West, launched a year later, and is considered by some to be the first rodeo.

March 9, 1886 — First National Bank established.

1887 — North Platte Waterworks Company started.

1892 — Electric light company organized, but goes out of business by 1895. New company organized in 1902.

April 7, 1893 — Great prairie fire sweeps into town and reaches Locust Street (now Jeffers), wiping out bottling works and creamery and 35 homes.

December, 1895 — Oliver W. Sizemore installed the first telephone in North Platte. First switchboard installed in the rear of his barber shop in 1896.

Sept. 8, 1889 — St. Patrick's School opens on Fourth Street in the parish's first frame church and in the convent.

March 4, 1901 — Col. William F. Cody selected to lead the parade in Washington, D.C. for the inauguration of President McKinley.

March 4, 1904 — University of Nebraska Agricultural Experiment Substation begins operation at North Platte. (The UNL West Central Research and Extension Center celebrated its 100th anniversary in 2004.)

May, 1905 — President Theodore Roosevelt's railroad car stops in North Platte and he delivers "a splendid speech."

May, 1908 — Federal building funds of $110,000 "engineered through Congress" by Congressman Moses P. Kinkaid. (This first post office building, completed in 1913 at Fifth and Jeffers, later became North Platte Junior College, then the Mid-Plains Community College area office. It was acquired by the City in 2001 with plans to renovate it for city offices and a community building.)

Sept. 23, 1908 — The Keith Theater opens. It was where the first all-talking movie was shown Dec. 26, 1928.

1911-1912 — Foundation of what later became the Chamber of Commerce organized. It was reorganized in 1920.

April 12, 1912 — Opening and dedication of new Carnegie Library. (Now the North Platte Children's Museum.)

Nov. 3, 1913 — New Union Pacific Roundhouse occupied.

June 16, 1916 — North Platte Country Club formed.

1916 — McDaid School completed.

1916 — Keith Neville of North Platte elected governor of Nebraska. The 32-year-old Democrat was called "the boy governor." He served a two-year term, 1917-1919.

1917 — "Massive brick building, two stories in height" erected on Front Street for fire station and city offices. Cost: $12,000. (Privately renovated, it now houses apartments and offices at Front and Vine).

1921 — North Platte Chamber of Commerce organizes private funding to buy land and build an airport.

Feb. 21, 1921 — Jack Knight flies the North Platte to Omaha leg of the first night air mail flight, then from Omaha to Iowa City and on to Chicago, helping establish a new transcontinental record and building support for an air mail service.

1929 — Jeffers Pavilion built by Union Pacific Employees Athletic Club as an open-air dance pavilion, later enlarged and enclosed.

July 13, 1929 — A white police officer called to stop an argument was shot and killed by a black man, who was in turn killed. Within hours, word spread that all the black people "had better get out of town."

July 5, 1930 — Radio station KGNF goes on the air, operating from a building constructed for that purpose at 1520 West 12th Street (now Rodeo Road). Call letters were changed to KODY on Dec. 13, 1943.

December, 1930 — Classes move into the new North Platte High School on West Second, replacing the downtown high school built in 1899.

Nov. 3, 1933 — Public Works Administration announces approval of the Sutherland Project and allots $7.5 million for its development. That would create Sutherland Reservoir and Lake Maloney and an extensive canal system for irrigation along with a hydro-power plant at North Platte.

1934 — Robert LeRoy Cochran, who had graduated from Brady High School and had been Lincoln County surveyor, and later State Highway Engineer, is elected governor. He would serve for three terms.

Nov. 5, 1935 — A dinner at the Pawnee Hotel celebrates completion of the last link to be paved in the Lincoln Highway (2-1/2 mile segment west of North Platte), giving the nation its first hard-surfaced transcontinental highway.

August 19, 1937 — Jeffers viaduct opens. Cost: $156,866.

Oct. 1, 1937 — William M. Jeffers, born in North Platte Jan. 2, 1876, becomes president of the Union Pacific Railroad, a post he would hold until retirement Feb. 1, 1946.

Dec. 25, 1941 — North Platte Canteen opens. Before its final day on April 1, 1946, volunteers would serve free food and smiles to more than six million service men and women.

1948 — Union Pacific builds first retarder or "hump yard" at North Platte. Cost: $3.5 million.

April, 1951 — Kirk Mendenhall elected mayor of North Platte, heading a slate organized to eliminate the prostitution and open gambling that had given the city a reputation as "Little Chicago." He appointed a new police chief, Charles Dick, and the "rooming houses" were closed.

November, 1952 — Robert B. Crosby of North Platte is elected governor of Nebraska. He would serve one term, then be defeated in a race for the U.S. Senate by Congressman Carl T. Curtis of Minden.

June 30, 1956 — Jeffers Pavilion, where many had danced to name bands of the big band era, destroyed by a fire which was ruled as arson. No one was ever identified as having set the fire.

Burned August 1949.

July 15, 1956 — The new Memorial Hospital at 715 South Jeffers is dedicated. The city purchased the building after Great Plains Regional Medical Center was built and with renovations and additions it became the Public Safety Building.

Nov. 21, 1956 — "After 20 years of talk" but no action, steps are taken to organize an industrial development corporation. J. L. "Roy" Keenan leads formation of what later became known as DEVCO.

Sept. 23, 1959 — Celebration at Thedford marks completion of paving on last segment of US Highway 83 (11 miles north of Stapleton) to be hard-surfaced. That made Highway 83 a paved road from Canada to Mexico. Promotion efforts were enhanced in 1994 with approval of the North American Free Trade Agreement (NAFTA) designed to remove barriers to trade between Canada, the United States, and Mexico.

July 28, 1960 — Chamber of Commerce and Historical Society leaders open drive to raise $37,500 for one-half the purchase price of a part of historic Scout's Rest Ranch. State Game, Forestation and Parks Commission matches that amount and makes the Cody home a state historical park.

Sept. 17, 1963 — North Platte State Bank opens. It later becomes North Platte National Bank, then Western Nebraska National Bank, then Wells Fargo Bank. The addition of an aggressive third bank contributed to changing a conservative lending policy that had at times handicapped the town's business growth.

June 24, 1965 — Buffalo Bill Ranch State Historical Park dedicated.

August 29, 1965 — Open house marks the start of North Platte Junior College in the former Post Office building at Fifth and Jeffers.

Sept. 22, 1966 — Interstate 80 opens to North Platte.

November, 1966 — North Platte selected as permanent home for statewide NEBRASKAland Days celebration by 4-3 vote of Game Commission. First year in North Platte to be 1968.

1968 — Eastbound hump, the new "Bailey Yard" completed, named for Union Pacific Railroad President Edd Bailey, who called North Platte home. Cost: $12.5 million.

September, 1968 — First classes of Mid-Plains Vocational Technical College start in temporary quarters in downtown North Platte. First classes on what is now North Campus of North Platte Community College were held in 1970.

April 22, 1971 — Formal opening of the new Union Pacific Diesel Repair Shop at North Platte. Cost: More than $10 million.

June 25, 1971 — Construction begins on $4 million Mall Shopping Center.

May 4, 1972 — North Platte gets $692,262 federal grant to begin downtown urban renewal program.

August 9, 1975 — New Great Plains Medical Center building dedicated, climaxing an effort that began in 1969. "Regional" was later added to the name.

Oct. 18, 1975 — The killing of six members of the Henry Kellie family in Sutherland sends shock waves through the community and sets in motion events that would lead to a landmark U.S. Supreme Court decision in an ongoing argument over freedom of the press and the right to a fair trial. The court's ruling on June 30, 1976 in Nebraska Press Association et al vs. Stuart effectively discouraged judicial censorship of the press in criminal proceedings.

Oct. 21, 1975 — Voters approve a nearly $10 million bond issue to build a new junior high, one new elementary school, new buildings or additions at six elementary schools.

April 6, 1976 — Recreation Center opens.

July 4, 1976 — Lincoln County Historical Society Museum dedicated.

July 20, 1980 — Dedication of new westbound hump yard at North Platte. Cost: $40.1 million.

July 27, 1981 — Willow Street viaduct construction begins. Dedicated in November, 1982. Cost "just over $2 million."

June 25, 1982 — Dedication of Nebraska Public Power District's Gerald Gentleman Power Station near Sutherland. Cost of Unit No. 1: $335 million; Unit No. 2, $287 million.

April 17, 1983 — Jeffers viaduct closed for widening. Reopened August 20, 1984.

March 3, 1987 — John Newburn dies at 101, leaving most of a nearly $2 million estate to the City of North Platte for park additions and improvements.

Nov. 1, 1989 — Buffalo Bill viaduct opens.

1994 — Iron Eagle Golf Course opens. Voters had approved construction of a municipal course on May 12, 1992, on land donated by the Glenn Chase family near the Newberry Road east access off Interstate-80.

Nov. 11, 1997 — Flying J Travel Plaza opens south of North Platte's east access off Interstate 80.

1997 — Life-size statue of William F. "Buffalo Bill' Cody comes from England to Cody Park.

Jan. 1, 1998 — New owners take over Camino Inn and begin renovation and new construction to create Quality Inn and Suites and Sandhills Convention Center.

Jan. 13, 1998 — First lunch served in new addition to North Platte Senior Center.

January, 1998 — Boys and Girls Home of Nebraska moves into new building at 2300 East Second St.

May 4, 2000 — Voters give 63 percent approval for $29 million bond issue to construct a new North Platte High School.

Sept. 19, 2001 — About 300 people gather at the Quality Inn to celebrate the announcement that Wal-Mart will build a $40 million distribution center at North Platte.

Sept. 3, 2002 — Doris Dotson cuts ribbon that marks the opening of the 12th Street-US 30 Bypass and North Platte's fifth viaduct.

May 26, 2003 — Memorial Day dedication ceremonies held for 20th Century Veterans Memorial in Iron Horse Park south of North Platte. Another ceremony on Veterans Day, Nov. 11, marks placement of the "Defenders of Liberty" statue by Ted Long. Fund-raising for the project continues.

August 29, 2003 — First classes held in new North Platte High School building. Dedication held Sept. 14.

Book Two

The Pivotal Campaign of 1951

1940s growth sets the stage
for change

The 1950 census gave North Platte a population of 15,433. That was a 24 percent increase from the 1940 count of 12,429. The city was growing, and restless.

The town's daily newspaper, the Telegraph-Bulletin, was becoming a leading voice for community improvements. Merger of two dailies, the Telegraph and the Bulletin, had taken place in 1946, when Joe W. Seacrest of Lincoln purchased the tabloid Bulletin and merged it with L. A. Kelly's Telegraph. Kelly remained as publisher, but Seacrest brought C. H. "George" Cooper to North Platte to manage the newspaper. Cooper brought to the newspaper a high degree of integrity and a strong sense of civic responsibility.

In 1948, voters approved a $987,000 bond issue for a new junior high school

C. H. "George" Cooper became general manager of the Telegraph-Bulletin after the merger of two competing dailies, the Telegraph and the Bulletin, in 1946. He guided the newspaper to new standards of quality journalism and community involvement.

and some additions and improvements to other school buildings. The vote was on April 6, and a page one editorial in the Telegraph-Bulletin April 7 was headlined "North Platte Goes Forward." The editor added:

By their action citizens of North Platte took a distinct step forward and served notice to other communities and the state at large that this city is determined to give the best educational facilities possible to our children.

The Telegraph-Bulletin had been vigorous in support of the

bond issue, both in editorials and in personal columns by Sports Editor Jim Kirkman and Sports writer Jim Cornwell.

Cornwell hit a not unfamiliar note in his column April 5, two days before the election, saying the issue "is very definitely in doubt."

North Platte has long been notorious for its group of "aginners" ..... The only way we who are wholeheartedly in favor of the bond issue, for what it will mean to our city, can combat this faction is to go to the voting places ourselves -- and vote "fer" our cause.

School Board President George Luedke emphasized community uses of the new building in a news story April 3.

The architects were instructed, he said, to plan the auditorium, gymnasium, cafeteria and other parts of the building which might be needed for community use so that they would be readily accessible.

Realizing the need for larger auditorium facilities, 1,200 seats have been planned for the main auditorium and several hundred stadium seats on the opposite side of the gym will serve to handle larger crowds for certain types of programs where scenery is not needed.....

Another point in favor of the bond issue was offered:

The Board of education today reaffirmed the previous announcement that the sale price of the present junior high school building would be applied to the bonded indebtedness of the new junior high school building. The site and building are valued in the neighborhood of $150,000.

That reference was to the Franklin Junior High building, located downtown at Fourth and Dewey. It had been built in 1917 next to the old high school building. After the new Adams Junior High was built in 1950 it was sold and became part of the Lincoln Plaza shopping area. That disappeared in turn to be replaced by a building for Western Nebraska National Bank, now Wells Fargo Bank.

The bond issue included funds for a modest addition to the high school building to house a vocational agriculture program. Improved facilities for the shop program were also programmed.

It seems clear the need for better sports facilities and for a larger community/school auditorium played a considerable part in public support of the bond issue. So, too, did the obvious need for the junior high to move from an antiquated facility in a busy downtown area. As the Telegraph emphasized in a March 23 editorial:

Anyone who is at all familiar with local school conditions will admit that the present Junior High School building is totally inadequate to take care of our growing needs. It is a firetrap and its location at the main corner of our business section and on U.S. Highway No. 30 presents a traffic hazard, to say nothing of the difficulty of teaching pupils with huge transport trucks rumbling along outside.

But as much as anything, the new junior high was a sign of a changing attitude in the community. The population growth of the 1940s had put pressure on school facilities, and meant new energy and new leadership.

Another example was a successful bond issue campaign in 1949 for a municipal swimming pool.

The campaign began officially with an announcement in the Telegraph-Bulletin on Sept. 12 that Ray Young had been named chairman of the committee to lead the drive in favor of the bond issue. Kirkman had been pushing for a swimming pool in his Telegraph-Bulletin sports columns long before that.

On Oct. 10, just before the election, he repeated arguments made previously in his "Dots and Dashes" column:

As long as North Platte fails to provide its citizens with safe, ample and modern swimming facilities, the cost will be paid off in the loss of lives.

....The existence of a muni swimming pool will not completely eliminate such tragedies, ... But the availability of a municipal swimming pool will eliminate the 'guilt complex' we all may have when such tragedies do occur.

But the real danger, as we see it, lies in the fact that the majority of North Platte young people are growing up in this area of manmade lakes and streams without even fundamental knowledge of swimming.

...A muni pool with its Red Cross swimming and life saving classes, will increase by tremendous numbers , the boys and girls in North Platte who will learn to feel at home in the water.....

Franklin School was built next to the high school in 1917. The high school was replaced by a new building at the west edge of town in 1930, but Franklin, at the busy downtown intersection of Fourth and Dewey, was still in use as a junior high in 1948. A successful bond issue election that year resulted in construction of Adams Junior High just west of the 1930 high school on West Second. After the new junior high was completed in 1950, the Franklin building housed retail shops and became part of the Lincoln Plaza Shopping Center. Western Nebraska National Bank began demolishing the shopping center in 1995 for construction of its new building, now Wells Fargo Bank.

"Swimming Pool Issue Is Passed By Wide Margin," the Telegraph-Bulletin reported on Wednesday, Oct. 12, 1949.

Unofficial totals were 2,000 for and 681 against the issue, almost a 3-1 margin. The proposal was for $74,000 in bonds. Although only 2,581 voted out of approximately 8,000 registered, the turnout was nearly as large as the previous spring's regular city election and more than voted two years before, the Telegraph-Bulletin noted. The newspaper also reviewed a history of problems and delays with the swimming pool project.

A bond issue of $61,000 was voted several years ago for the purpose of constructing a municipal pool. However, it was found that with rising costs, it was impossible to build the pool for that amount of money.

Bids were again taken this past summer and it was found that the low bid was still over double the amount of money available for the purpose.

*The bond issue voted Tuesday will make about $135,000
available for the pool. Construction will probably not be started
until early spring .... A completely modern bathhouse and pool
meeting AAU specification is planned.*

Ray Young's pool campaign committee had included a nice
mixture of longtime residents and relative newcomers. Young
was co-owner of Young's Sporting Goods. Other members of the
committee included Mrs. Verne Taylor, sister of Telegraph
Publisher L. A. Kelly; R. L. Getty, Telegraph editor; John
Alexander, manager of KODY radio; Otto Oakes, superintendent
of Schools; Lorraine Orr, Russ Langford, Leo Anderson, Dr. H.
K. Young and others.

The successful junior high bond issue in 1948 and the swimming pool proposal in 1949 helped set the stage for major civic
progress in 1950 and beyond. The mixture of old and new leadership, proving that citizen action could make a difference, probably helped build the base of the city government reform campaign of 1951.

1951 election changed North Platte

This was a classic local election campaign, maybe the most interesting and significant North Platte has ever experienced.

I came to town as a young reporter in 1952, so I missed the fireworks, but I heard the stories.

The most frequent story I heard was that a newspaper headline about high school boys being patrons of the brothels had finally stirred the community to action. Certainly it helped mobilize public opinion, but the reform movement was already under way.

It apparently began with a small group formed quietly early in the year. Chris Rosenberg, a 30-year-old owner of an insurance agency, was a member.

He suggested Kirk Mendenhall as the ideal candidate for mayor "because he operated a business impervious to any business pressure." Mendenhall was a partner in Central Nebraska Packing Co., a horse meat packing plant not dependent on local markets. Rosenberg became Mendenhall's campaign manager.

Announcement of the Citizens Committee candidates

Kirk Mendenhall was elected mayor in 1951 in a campaign to eliminate wide-open gambling and prostitution, and succeeded in spite of strong opposition from some business leaders and threats against his family. That issue and others resulted in his defeat for a second term, but he continued to serve the community in other ways, especially as a leader in the Boy Scout organization, until his death at 81 in August, 1994.

Courtesy Sue Mendenhall Rutt

appeared in the North Platte Telegraph-Bulletin on Feb. 12, five days before the headline highlighting the involvement of high school students.

The announcement named three co-chairmen of the committee (C. W. Heming, Dr. G. F. Waltemath, and W. D. Newberry) and emphasized the business background of the candidates. There was only a veiled reference to the vice issue:

The three co-chairmen also said the group intends to expand its ranks during future meetings to include all citizens who share the belief that North Platte is entitled to and should have better city government in its many and varied phases of operation, including the strict enforcement of existing laws.

It is a story Jim Kirkman might have written. His primary duties at the newspaper were in advertising and sports, but he also sometimes wrote news on issues he was interested in. He was deeply involved in the Citizens Committee. Working mostly behind the scenes, he would continue to lead groups seeking to encourage and support strong candidates for many years before finally becoming a candidate for mayor himself.

The story most people remembered later when they described the 1951 campaign appeared under a four-column lead headline in the Telegraph-Bulletin on Saturday, Feb. 17:

"Houses Of Prostitution Ordered/Closed by County Attorney," it said. The subhead added: ***"High School/Students/Are Involved; McIntosh Declares/Order Will Be/Enforced to Letter."*** The story began:

Six houses of prostitution in North Platte have been ordered "to close and get out," County Attorney Jim McIntosh told the Telegraph-Bulletin this morning.

"If we discover any others open they will get the same treatment," McIntosh declared.

"They have been getting by with murder," the county attorney added, figuratively speaking.

One of the reasons for the close order, according to McIntosh is the fact that an investigation shows such houses are involved in patronage of high school students.

The county attorney stated that he, together with Sheriff Barney Discoe and Police Chief Mason called on the Como,

Glendale, Star and Broadmoor rooms yesterday and notified them to "close and get out," and that notice was served today on the Rex rooms and the rooms above the 215 club.

"We intend to follow through and see that this order is carried out," McIntosh declared.

Chief of Police Ernest Mason in a statement to the Telegraph-Bulletin said his department is cooperating with the county attorney's office and sheriff and declared a check will be maintained to see that the order is enforced....

A page-one editorial accompanying the news story closed with these paragraphs:

It is time that the laws against prostitution be enforced....

We don't believe the people of North Platte will continue to tolerate the wide open condition so brazen that it caters to teenagers in our high school. We hope the pressure of public opinion continues long enough to support a permanent cleanup of such conditions.

Kirkman and C. H. "George" Cooper, the general manager of the newspaper, were supporting the reform movement. The publisher and 50 percent owner, Louis A. Kelly, remained loyal to his longtime friend, Mayor Sydney P. McFarland. So while the Citizens Committee generated news pointing to the need for reform, the Telegraph-Bulletin editorials favored the existing administration. Kirkman was almost certainly writing the hard-hitting advertisements for the reform slate.

Looking back later, Kirkman figured that situation could have gotten him fired. But Kelly liked Kirkman. The two had an understanding that neither one would read the other's copy before it appeared in the paper.

News emphasis on vice conditions had begun even earlier. A page one Telegraph-Bulletin story on Friday, Jan. 26, 1951, was headlined ***"Prostitution Said 'Brazen' in North Platte."*** It quoted the Omaha World-Herald:

In one of a series of feature stories the World Herald today said "Flagrant and brazen prostitution in North Platte and to a lesser degree in Omaha seriously counteracts the effectiveness of the entire venereal disease program in Nebraska.

"This is another statement from the Christ J. Petrow report on state health work. It is an example used to show how the State Health Department has failed to gain needed cooperation at the local level ....

The Omaha newspaper quoted the Petrow report as saying

"There can be no excuse for the prevalence of open, organized prostitution in Nebraska."

About 100 thousand dollars is spent annually in combating these diseases.

"Rapid treatment centers and clinics have been set up in Omaha and other cities of Nebraska; free drugs are made available to all physicians; trained investigators roam the state .... pamphlets, movies, lectures and public health education and information are made available as a public service.

"Yet a few apa-

Jim Kirkman's talent for designing effective ads played a role in the reform election of 1951, and Kirkman was also undoubtedly working with the reform committee as well. From at least the 1950s on he spearheaded a group dedicated to finding and encouraging qualified candidates for public office, and finally became a two-term mayor himself after retiring as publisher of the Telegraph.

thetic doctors and situations such as exist in North Platte are obstructing the effectiveness of the program and providing a health menace."

Mayor Sidney P. McFarland in a statement to the *Telegraph-Bulletin* this morning, said:

"Mr. Petrow's statements about the state board of health and the city of North Platte were based on a survey made two years ago, were not up to date and do not reflect present conditions.

"We have been working very closely with the state department of health and they have given us complete cooperation. Venereal disease has gone way down since the gambling 'crackdown' in the city and the state.

"I have contacted Dr. Ryder of the State Department of Health and he assures me there is no reason for North Platte to have any special attention."

On the day after the Citizens Committee announcement of its slate of candidates, McFarland announced he would not be a candidate for re-election. *The Telegraph-Bulletin* on April 13 carried this from McFarland:

"I wish to thank my friends who are endeavoring to have me run for Mayor and I take this opportunity to say that I am not a candidate for any political office nor do I have any political ambitions. I also want to express my gratitude for the loyalty and support you have given me and I hope I have done justice to your expectations."

An editorial on page one praised McFarland.

Mayor McFarland to Not Be
Candidate -- Enviable Record

The announcement that Sydney P. McFarland will not again be a candidate for mayor at the city election on April 3, which immediately follows this editorial, comes as both a surprise and regret to his many friends. Mayor McFarland has served this city faithfully for three terms. He has given freely of his time to city affairs. He was never too busy to talk and discuss civic matters with the citizens. He leaves the city government in the best of financial condition. His terms as mayor has (sic) seen a most prosperous growth in North Platte's population development.

Mayor McFarland has fathered many city improvements such as the recent ordinance requiring additions to the city to pay for their own improvements before being taken into the city. He sponsored the municipal swimming pool and was mayor during the greater part of the life of the Municipal Light and Power company. He has also worked hard for the development of our municipal airport, keeping it up-to-date as one of the best airports in Nebraska.

The citizens of North Platte owe Mayor McFarland a vote of thanks for his untiring work as head of our city government.

Always looking toward the best interests of the city as a whole he never deviated from his position for any particular group. His record should be a source of satisfaction to him in retiring from the office. He was not only mayor on council nights, but he spent long hours every day at the job, following a full day's work in his position with the railroad.

The editorial surely was written or inspired by publisher Lou Kelly. Robert F. Getty, the long-time editor, was also supportive of McFarland.

The Telegraph on Feb. 15, 1951 reported on a Citizens Committee meeting the evening before at the Pawnee Hotel. Members of a "policy committee" were identified as Gerald Gentleman, J. J. Swanson, George Cooper, J. M. McNeil and George Dent. W. D. "Twist" Newberry was named chairman.

The Feb. 22 *Telegraph-Bulletin* reported, *"friends of Mayor Sidney P. McFarland,"* had filed petitions naming him as a candidate for mayor. McFarland *"again declared today he definitely is not a candidate."* (The newspaper often spelled McFarland's first name as "Sidney" or "Sid" but "Sydney" is correct.)

By March 2, McFarland had changed his mind. *"Mayor Sydney P. McFarland is definitely a candidate for re-election at the coming city election,"* The Telegraph-Bulletin reported.

The newspaper reported in its March 13 edition on a meeting of the Citizens Committee the evening before:

A cleanup of gambling and prostitution in North Platte was promised last night by the Citizens Committee candidates in the city election.

Their stand on the two issues struck an enthusiastic response from an overflow crowd of approximately 250 persons in the courtroom at the county courthouse. Many stood at doorways in the hall to hear the speakers.

"North Platte can get along without a single prostitute in town and I hope they're plumb out of the county," Kirk Mendenhall, candidate for mayor, said.

In his address Mendenhall chided city officials who *"assure us on various occasions that everything is closed up tight and that all laws are being enforced.*

"Recent disregard of the law has become so brazen that houses of prostitution who frown upon the city's ordinances also dis-

regard the laws of human decency by catering to high school boys."

Mendenhall continued that *"Apparently law enforcement has been so lax that the activities which have existed have been joked about....."*

The same edition of the *Telegraph* carried a letter from Bill Owens, 1610 West First, outlining what would become the McFarland campaign's main themes.

Is North Platte such a terrible place to live?

As an adopted son of North Platte, let me tell you how I feel about it. My work has made it necessary for me, and my family, to live in several towns in Nebraska, Wyoming and Kansas since the war. Three years ago we came to North Platte assuming this, as other towns, would be a difficult place in which to get acquainted. North Platte's mantle was spread -- its Newcomer service, its parks and picnic areas its nearby lakes and rivers, its beautiful churches and schools, its year round sports activities, its modern stores and theaters seemed to welcome us; but most wonderful of all were its people.

My wife, my children and I have felt from our first few moments that we have found home -- a city we want to remain a part of the rest of our lives.

During these years we have found North Platte also has its untidy side -- as do all towns. No less, and certainly no greater. In three short years we have seen the building of new churches, of large stores, of a beautiful new swimming pool, of a magnificent junior high school. We have enjoyed the benefits of its year round sports program, second to none. We have seen how a city can be run within its means; how a municipal power and light plant can operate so efficiently it is becoming a model to be copied....

Our young people of North Platte are no different from those of 20 years ago, or those of any other town -- no better, and certainly no worse. Those who will find bad, will find it at all costs and the penalty suffered by the good is no less severe because of the example.

I love North Platte and I am sure I express the feeling of many North Platters, native and otherwise, when I say that recent statements about it being an "evil, notorious, ill run city" are resented....

Owens, a Union Pacific employee, became a leading voice in the group that unseated Mendenhall in the election two years later.

R. F. "Bub" Easter, countered with a letter to the editor two days later.

Unlike Bill Owens, who tells us he came to North Platte just three years ago, I have been a resident of this city for many, many years.

I too am proud of North Platte because it has been very much a part of my life.

However, again apparently unlike Mr. Owens, I know how the North Platte citizens have happened to obtain the many fine facilities Mr. Owens was so eager to mention in his letter to the editor....

Would he presume to tell us that North Platte's parks and picnic areas, its nearby lakes and rivers, its beautiful churches and schools, its year-around sports activities and its modern stores and theaters could by any stretch of the imagination be the result of the existence of houses of prostitution or commercial gambling.

North Platte's progress in school expansion, park expansion, etc., with rare exception, was instigated and then promoted by the same North Platte citizens who are presenting the "Citizens Committee" slate for election. The very things that Mr. Owens, through his own admission, enjoys in North Platte did not come about by accident, but were the results of the imagination, promotion, and work of the same citizens who, in the most part, are seeking a new city administration.

How do I know? I know, Mr. Owens, because I have been a member of that group. The group which presented as its candidates North Platte's present board of education. The group which cooperated with the P.T.A. and got behind the school bond issues that found popular acceptance. The group that put over the municipal swimming pool bond issues   which had previously failed without organized civic support.

These accomplishments did not come by accident, nor were they the result of present administration leadership.

Has Mayor McFarland finally decided that a youth center is a worthwhile project when upon repeated occasions he has expressed the fact that these facilities were not necessary when he was a boy and shouldn't be necessary now?

Would Mayor McFarland take credit for a swimming pool that the citizens themselves promoted, and then were sold down the river when the city administration refused to follow the recommendations of the group which successfully promoted the bond issue, with this pool then costing the taxpayers almost double because of avoidable delays which finally required a second bond issue to obtain sufficient money to pay for the cost of the pool?

Would Mayor McFarland deny that he cast the vote breaking the tie after the city council was deadlocked on the issue so that the low bidder did not receive the contract to construct the muni swimming pool?

..... Not one of the many advantages Mr. Owens mentioned in his letter were the result of either Mayor McFarland's origination or leadership ....

"MAKE A FINE CITY BETTER!" trumpeted the large type in a March 21 advertisement for the Citizen Committee slate of candidates. It followed with campaign themes, including a description of positive aspects of the community but with emphasis on the need to do something about the key issue:

Important Railroad Center, Strong Churches, Up To Date School System, Wide Trade Area, Active Business Community.

But -- For Too Many Years ...

-- We have tried to look away from organized vice and gambling

-- We have tolerated conditions we could not recommend to our children

WHO IS TO BLAME?

-- Not just the present city administration -- it has permitted a condition that has persisted through many years. But custom does not justify defiance of law.

-- You and I are to blame. We shall have as good government as we demand, as poor as we tolerate.

Pictures of Mendenhall and the four city council candidates followed. A box within the ad urged:

"Let's Make North Platte Better! -- For the first time in many years a group of candidates have come out flat-footedly for honest law enforcement in North Platte. Give Them A Chance!"

An opposition advertisement March 24 followed with a *"STATEMENT OF FACTS."*

It was written as a letter from incumbent Mayor Sydney P. McFarland and began:

....There have been many rumors and untruths spread in this campaign. Worse than that, there have been half truths, which can be more vicious and result in smear to a lower degree than untruths. I have not indulged in such tactics, and I will not, at any time, do so....

McFarland continued: *"I have always been interested in the home owners and taxpayers of this City, and I have followed a policy of economy in matters of City Government..."*

Under *"Financial Condition,"* McFarland listed paving and sewer improvements, *"1,577 books have been purchased for your library, 21 blocks of new mercury vapor street lighting, new street markers and other improvements."*

I have always been interested in young people and the activities of our youth. I have been anxious to promote anything to help these young people grow up in a better world. It was my privilege to obtain certain hard-to-get materials for school improvements, and put up the first baseball backstops and basketball racks on every school ground in the City at no cost to the school district or the City. I have made a careful study of the rumors passed around recently regarding our school children, and I am convinced that our children and teen agers are not as guilty as some profess....

Certainly, I am opposed to prostitution and gambling, and any violation of the laws and ordinances of the city of North Platte and our Government. Having been identified with the city for the past 14 years, I also realize the difficulty of the enforcement of some of the laws. However, it is not an impossibility and will require the efforts of all the citizens....

A letter from Chris Rosenberg in the March 25 *Telegraph-Bulletin* pointed to a campaign tactic that was, and still is at times, a feature of this railroad town's political landscape:

The newspaper reflected the town's split personality on the issues. Jim Kirkman was probably writing the ads and helping plot strategy for the Citizens Committee. George Cooper may have been one of the initiators of the reform campaign. But the day before the election, Telegraph-Bulletin editor Bob Getty wrote this:

As often is the case, the editor was partly right and partly
wrong. The McFarland administration had given the town about
what it deserved as long as a majority of citizens chose not to
look too hard at what was going on. It would also be one thing to
talk about cracking down on gambling and prostitution, another
thing to actually do it.

But North Platte had reached a major turning point. In this
election, a majority voted for change.

'New' leadership sparked Cleanup campaign in 1951

The reform campaign of 1951 was powered by relatively young leaders, some with deep roots in the community and some a part of the influx of new residents during the 1940s.

One of the youngest was Chris Rosenberg, who was only 30 in the spring of 1951, but had been running his insurance business for 10 years. He was born near Bignell in southeast Lincoln County but grew up in North Platte and left college when he was 19 to take over the business after his father died in 1940.

Jim Kirkman moved to town with his parents when he was a high school youngster in 1924. He was 40 when the 1951 election campaign began, with 25 years of involvement in the town as sports writer, advertising salesman and promoter of various sports and entertainment events.

Bob Crosby, a North Platte native, turned 40 during the reform campaign.

Gerald Gentleman, a legend in the development of public power in Nebraska, had lived in North Platte since about 1933. He was 57 in 1951.

E. W. "Ed" Johannesen turned 45 during the campaign in which he was elected to the city council. He had opened his insurance business in North Platte in 1945.

W. D. "Twist" Newberry was 42. He had moved to North Platte in 1937 as property manager for his father-in-law, Keith Neville. Newberry was originally from Texas. He had married Frances Neville in 1934.

Dale L. Keeney, 33 when he was elected to the council in 1951, was a Union Pacific freight agent, and a native of Hershey who had worked for the UP since 1935, with time out for Navy service in the Pacific during World War II.

C. W. "Bill" Heming came to North Platte in 1947. He owned the Bill Heming Lincoln-Mercury auto agency. He was a Chappell native who graduated from the University of Nebraska in 1941 and served in the Army Air Corps from 1943 to 1945. He was married to Mildred Beatty, daughter of a North Platte attorney. Heming was 32 when he was elected to the council on the reform slate.

Vern Lyons was 40 when he was elected to the council in 1951. He moved to North Platte in 1930, working at the E. A. Gamble Market until he purchased it in 1943 and named it Lyons IGA Foodliner.

C. H. "George" Cooper, general manager of the Telegraph-Bulletin and a strong supporter of the reform movement, came to North Platte in the fall of 1946. He had just turned 48 when the reform campaign began.

The incumbent mayor, Sydney P. McFarland, was only 54 but had already served three two-year terms as mayor (two terms from 1943-1947 and a third from 1949-51) so was clearly part of the "old guard."

Louis A. Kelly, also 54 in 1951, was a friend of McFarland since high school days. Kelly had been employed at the Telegraph, owned by his father, since 1919 and had been publisher since 1935, continuing as publisher and co-owner after the Telegraph became the Telegraph-Bulletin in 1946.

Reform slate wins,
then the job begins

The slate of candidates pledged to end wide-open prostitution and gambling in North Platte won the 1951 city election on April 3.

".... the citizens committee, with their reform platform, brought out the largest number of votes of any city election to date," The Lincoln County Tribune reported on April 5. *"The newly elected slate gained their popularity on their reform platform of a clean-up of prostitution and gambling."*

"The Citizens Committee carried all precincts, and by 10:30 p.m. Tuesday, Mendenhall had run up such an impressive lead over McFarland, that the present mayor conceded defeat with only complete returns from two precincts."

The Tribune had Mendenhall with 2,879 votes to McFarland's 1,559 in unofficial returns. Ed Johannesen beat Ed Helstrom in the First Ward 698-325. Bill Heming beat T. F. Crawford in the Second Ward 965-522. Dale Keeney took the Third Ward seat over write-in candidate Donald E. Wright 633-198. Vern Lyons won in the Fourth Ward with 470 votes to 216 for Kenneth Weinberger and 155 for Thomas Smith Jr.

City Clerk L. E. Mehlmann, Police Judge Claude DeLany, and school board candidates States and Waltemath were unopposed.

A column called *"From The Editor's Notebook"* in the same issue of the Tribune congratulated the new city officers and added these comments:

"There are many things that these men have to take into consideration when they assume their new duties as head of North Platte....

"The citizens, too, have a lot to consider and that is the fact that this group of men nor any other group can make some of the changes which they pledge themselves to make overnight; It'll take time, and the help of all the citizens to work out the problems which face this city.

"But their city clean-up is only a part of their program, we predict a bright future for North Platte under the guidance of these young progressive business men, who have gotten off to a fine start by having the complete confidence of a majority of our citizens."

The new mayor and council members took office April 10 and Mendenhall promptly announced some changes. Capt. Millard Calhoun was named interim chief of police, replacing Ernie Mason, who *"would remain on the force on a temporary basis."*

Mendenhall was quoted as saying *"voters indicated they wanted a change in law enforcement practices."* Mendenhall also appointed Bob Crosby as city attorney, replacing Don Lowe. Clarence F. Frazier, a hold-over council member, was elected council president.

The Tribune editor's prediction that the cleanup wouldn't happen overnight proved true. The search for a new police chief lasted until August. In the meantime there was little overt action, some signs of impatience, and a hint that the election itself may have had some effect.

Maurice "Morie" Cotton had come to the weekly Lincoln County Tribune as editor and general manager in November, 1950. His column, "From The Editor's Notebook," touched on the cleanup issue frequently. In his May 17 issue, he wrote:

Speaking of the houses of prostitution, we have this to say. We know definitely, that these houses are not operating as openly as they were in the past. Rumors have it, that the houses are going full blast....they are not!

A stranger recently made a visit to each of the houses in this city, and he could not make a direct contact with a single woman.

We do not believe that prostitution has been eliminated by any means in North Platte .... this week's rumor has it stated this way:

"If a man is looking for a pay girl, he has to have a very definite contact. If he doesn't have it then he will not make any progress. The contacts are made in various public spots and are not apt to be made until late evening .... almost any time after 11 o'clock."

Where these professionals do business is questionable. Some speculate that they have moved to residential sections. Others say they have never moved. We do not know, but we are confident that this vice will never be completely eliminated until every person in this city cooperates with the law and helps to make this city a "hot spot" for these women.

Charles R. Dick was sworn in as police chief by Mayor Mendenhall on August 2, 1951. He came from Vancouver, WA, where he had been a deputy in the Clark County Sheriff's Department for more than 10 years. He had been a captain in the department for eight years, and had headed the personnel department. The Tribune story on August 2 mentioned as one of the new chief's *"top qualifications"* his work with juveniles.

Dick had been born and raised a near neighbor to North Platte, in Frontier County, leaving for the west coast in 1936, the Tribune reported. He had a sister and brother-in-law living in North Platte.

The Tribune expressed some impatience in an August 15 "About Town" column.

The new chief of police, Charles Dick, is a busy man these days. He has a lot of hot irons in the fire, but he let one of the hottest irons go out during the past week. The major clean-up campaign of the city, dropped about a hundred points , when the department failed to act on a hot tip. It seems to us that some of the citizens around town might lose faith in this promised campaign, if something doesn't happen soon.

There was action to report in the Tribune's August 23 "About Town" column.

Last week end brought more activity from the North Platte police department than has been brought to light in many a day. Not only did the local department make raids within the city limits, but the sheriff's department got in a healthy lick down Brady way. One $100 fine was collected on a bootlegging charge, and others picked up during the raids were released on bail bond. The Nebraska Liquor Control Commission had deputies in on the deal. We wonder if they spearheaded this "splurge" or if it was all figured out locally? We also wonder why the Rex Rooms, in particular, were chosen for one of the Sunday raids? At any rate the action is highly commendable and it looks as though a general clean-up campaign might be in the making.

Morie Cotton took another jab at the police department in his Oct. 4 "About Town" column, along with a reference to one of the town's legendary criminal figures.

One of North Platte's unwanted characters finally went the way of all law-breakers. Recently an announcement was made that "Blackie" Robinson, who not so many weeks ago freely roamed the streets of our town, was picked up by the FBI in connection with a bank robbery, which also involved the famous Kitts....

Speaking of unwanted characters, it seems as though we still have a few around town, although reports say "we're clean." The police department is doing a pretty good job in enforcing traffic laws, in marking parking places, and in keeping the high school drivers in line, but their big job hasn't had much push. We wonder if it's ever going to get under way. Recent reports say we are back in the "pre-election stage." About town knows very definitely that all is not under control "about town."

A Monday, Oct. 8, 1951 story in the North Platte Telegraph-Bulletin began:

"Prostitution is over in North Platte," Police Chief Charles Dick told four suspected operators of houses of ill repute Saturday.

Chief Dick's action came as a result of information he has received and uncovered that houses of prostitution were running "wide open" in North Platte, he said today.

On a routine check, Dick warned the reputed operators that prostitution is finished here. Raids would be made if the operators did not comply with city and state laws regarding prostitution and the keeping of disorderly houses, Dick added.

Within minutes of his visit to the four well-known "rooming houses," a "girl" telephoned a clothing store and ordered a set of luggage, presumably for an extended trip.

The Lincoln County Tribune reported the event more extensively in its Oct. 11 edition under the headline: "City Clean-up Campaign Reached/New Climax Saturday Afternoon."

The long-awaited clean-up campaign promised by the new city administration reached a climax Saturday afternoon when

Chief Charles Dick, Assistant Chief Millard Calhoun, and two members of the press went calling on four "rooming houses" in the downtown district. In no uncertain terms the two police officers told the managers of the "suspected hotels" or their employees that "this was it." Several of the hired maids were advised to leave town without delay by Chief Dick.....

The big blow-off started with a Dewey street stop as Dick and Calhoun, followed by the press made their surprise visit. The manager of the house extended an invitation to come "into her parlor." She also obligingly at the chief's suggestion, called in her two "maids." Both girls were from Omaha, and one of them said she had been in North Platte since June of this year. The other was a newcomer. She said she had only arrived on Friday night.

The manager of the hotel said she would guarantee that both of her helpers would be on the first train out of town. The elderly manager of the hotel said things had been rough, that she had been forced to borrow some money, and that one of the girls had come in to help out ....

This tour ended a long period of watchful waiting and investigation by the department concerning the activity of some hotels in North Platte, and it is assumed that all "shady activities," if there were any would come to a screeching halt.

We can probably mark October 6, 1951 as the "official" date when open prostitution and gambling was closed down in North Platte. Morie Cotton referred to it again in his final column before he moved on at the end of the year. It is likely he was one of the "press" that accompanied the two police officers on that Saturday afternoon, and a Telegraph-Bulletin reporter was the other.

There had been similar "raids" and warnings before, without much visible effect. This one seemed to stick. Possibly the reform campaign with its public focus in the newspapers had indeed turned public opinion around. What had been tolerated for decades, while "respectable" citizens simply looked the other way, was no longer acceptable.

Mendenhall's integrity and toughness probably had something to do with convincing the rooming house operators that this crack-down would be different. Councilman Ed Johannesen recalled later that there had been a steady but quiet pressure aimed at discouraging and embarrassing patrons of the establish-ments. Profits may have started to shrink, and business opera-tions may have become increasingly difficult, from the time the reform administration took office.

There were still sinners among us, as there always are. But commercial vice and the temptations to government corruption that accompany it no longer thrived. North Platte was ready for a new era.

Raids don't work,
steady pressure does

In a recorded interview with Zoe Ackerman in April, 1978, Ed Johannesen provided insights into North Platte's casual acceptance of open prostitution before 1951, and to the methods employed to discourage the houses of prostitution after the reform election.

Johannesen told Ackerman: *"One of the things that bothered me after going into the real estate business, which was 1945, was people would come to town and they'd look around for houses and then they would say 'we've heard about the gambling dens and houses of prostitution, do you know where they are?' And of course I knew where they were, so we would drive by them and point them out. At first it was embarrassing, however when I found out how people just wanted to satisfy their curiosity, it didn't bother me."*

Johannesen said he had gone to a meeting at which "a group of fellas wanted to clean up the town, and I ended up promising to accept the nomination as a councilman for my ward. I kind of blame Jimmy Kirkman for that. I told him I wanted nothing to do with it, but Kirkman talked me into it."

"There were quite a few people and some of them rather prominent who said you couldn't clean up the town, that people wanted this kind of a town with gambling and houses of prostitution and that we were to remain part of the old west. And that North Platte would lose a lot of business if the town was cleaned up.

"I think I was rather naïve. I thought it was going to be an easy job. I thought we'd raid the places and close them down.

"However, after we got into it there were more problems than appeared on the surface. So we went to the FBI, who cooperated with us, and advised us not to raid the places because generally we'd get beat in court. So we sometimes put plain clothing {police} out at a place and when the men would come out they'd stop them and ask what they were doing in a house of ill repute. If they gave them a little static, sometimes they would take them

to the police station and ask that somebody come and vouch for them. And I {participated in those stakeouts} several times at midnight and after. And I was threatened three or four times, that if we didn't lay off of them, my wife wouldn't know me when I got home.

"But once we got into it we just about had to stay. Having been in business a while, some of the people running these places were customers of mine. The lady who ran the Broadmoor Hotel, which was a house of ill repute, had purchased four or five properties from me. Mr. Hart, who was suspected of being a bank robber .... had purchased four or five properties from me. So I sat in a position that was a little hard to handle when you start to push on those people.

"When I was on the council I believe we raided two places. One was the Broadmoor Rooms or Broadmoor Hotel when the owner or manager took a vacation to California. Of course their attorney represented her right quick and we didn't get much done on that. And the raid that I took part in was when we raided Margie's Place, a chicken dinner and bootleg place. It was not successful because apparently they had been tipped off we were coming.

"Through the assistance of the FBI and the American Health Association as well as officers from the McCook Air Base, we were able to settle things down at first. Then as pressure became greater on the people running the houses of ill repute, they would move out of town."

Later in the interview, Johannesen added:

"I'll never forget the morning after my election, one of the madams whom I had sold three or four properties to came to my office and said, 'Ed are you going to raid me? If you do I'll have a heart attack and you'll be sorry.' But I wasn't in any mood to discuss it with her so we closed that conference in a hurry."

Some schoolboys were visitors, not customers

Another account from someone who had been a schoolboy during the days before the crackdown on vice came to me in an e-mail letter from Dick Dunn after he had read something I had written on the subject.

Dunn graduated from North Platte High School in 1948 and after service in the Marines and education at the University of Nebraska became a leading architect and civic leader in North Platte. At the time of this letter he was retired from the faculty of Colorado State University and living at Fort Collins, Colorado. On March 9, 2004, Dunn wrote me:

"The one thing you did not mention was the 'mafia' influence/control of the major houses of prostitution. The girls were moved here from Chicago or Omaha and after a few weeks, at most, were moved on to Denver or Cheyenne.

"This is first hand information as six of us used to visit the Brodbeck rooms on nights they were not busy. The madam thought it was important that the girls have contact with non-customers and the rule was we could not take the girls into the rooms nor could we arrange dates away from the 'house.'

"It worked great and we were all surprised how the younger ones seemed almost like 'the girl next door.' They talked about how they got into the business and how their location was controlled by the mafia, although I never remember that word being used.

"We discovered how much control the criminal element had both in North Platte and at the state level. This would have been in the late 1940's, after the war. We had a teenage club downtown that was located just West of Hirschfeld's when they were on the corner of 6th and Dewey.

"It was run as a private club by a man and his daughter and we paid monthly dues to belong. It was great with cold drinks, sandwiches, snacks, etc.. There was a juke box and dance floor. I remember a ping-pong table and maybe a pool table .... One day the manager announced we were being closed down as the building owner was leasing the building to a 'group' who were going to open an upscale restaurant and bar.

"We organized the teenagers and maybe a hundred of us appeared at the City Council meeting to protest the liquor license. They listened to our arguments, including that this was the only place in town that was designated for teenagers, and then voted to approve the license.

"We thought this was strange but an attorney advised us to take our protest to the State Liquor Commission hearing in Lincoln. We had several car loads that went to Lincoln and we

had several university students from North Platte that joined us. The State Liquor Commissioners listened, promised to take our concerns under advisement, and a few days later it was announced that the license was approved. At that point, our club was on a day to day lease and the day after the license was approved we were shut down and the remodeling began.

"We were hearing rumors that it would not be a good idea to picket or carry our protest any further, but we really did not realize that there may have been 'mafia' influence until after the restaurant was operating. People had noticed and commented on the big limousines that were showing up downtown shortly after New Years. Mary and I were having dinner at the restaurant one night about that time and our waitress apologized for a delay in the food service. She explained there was a large group in the meeting room and their body guards were overflowing into the dining room.

"I looked around and even back then you knew these huge lugs were not local. I asked the waitress where they were from and she answered Chicago, Denver, Cheyenne, Omaha, and where-ever. She shook her head and said that she didn't think it was a good idea to talk about them....

"A short time later my Dad told me he had been visiting with the local FBI agent, Bill Green, and Bill had asked him to keep an eye on the two story house in the next block (that would be the ten hundred block on West A) as there seemed to be a lot of out of state cars visiting in the neighborhood. Green was specific that if Dad could write down license plates without being observed it would be a big help. Later, a bank robber escaped from jail in Omaha and after he was caught in Colorado it came to light that he had stayed at the house on West A."

Reform is one thing, governing something else

The drama of the most successful vice cleanup in the city's history was followed by the task of dealing with mundane matters that plague city councils everywhere: garbage collection, loose dogs, traffic problems.

Postwar America was changing and North Platte was no exception. The swimming pool in Cody Park opened. The Country Club was talking about replacing sand greens with grass. The state was eager to build a new National Guard armory at North Platte if the city would come up with the land. Bob Crosby was elected governor of Nebraska and Dwight Eisenhower won the presidential election. Americans were worried about Communists and polio. But few things stir up the citizens like a change in garbage pickup.

Just such a change that would haunt Mendenhall and the new council members started with action by McFarland and the old council.

A Telegraph-Bulletin story on Jan. 3, 1951 reported:

The city may soon be operating its own garbage collection system. This became evident at last night's City Council meeting when it was made known that an ordinance is being prepared to put such a system into effect....

"Considerable time was spent discussing the city's planned venture into the garbage collection business," the Telegraph-Bulletin reported Jan. 17 in another council meeting story.

In the last business session before McFarland and four council members left office, the council *"set in motion the long-considered plans to institute a city-owned garbage collection system,"* the Telegraph-Bulletin reported on April 5.

The Council decided to go ahead and placed an order with the Iowa Supply Company for three Packmaster garbage collection boxes, although a garbage ordinance had not yet been passed. The time element was the reason for hastening the action.

It also instructed the city clerk to advertise for bids on truck cabs and chassis, to be considered at the May 8 meeting.

Councilman T. F. Crawford, who with Dr. Joel Anderson and C. F. Frazier has conducted a survey of collection systems, reported that the city would need to charge residents $1.25 monthly to make it work here. He added that the city would have to take over all collection in the residential areas.

He praised the new system highly as safer and more sanitary. "No burning of trash," he said, "the alleys are cleaner." He pointed out that from seven to 12 fires a year are caused here by burning trash.

The present contract with a private collector expires July 1. The Packmasters will cost the city $4,440 each.

Trouble started the very next day when the headline was: ***"Protest City's/Order to Buy/Refuse Trucks."***

Attorney George Dent, a former mayor, had presented a letter to the city clerk on behalf of W. H. Nielsen, owner of the North Platte Chevrolet dealership, challenging the purchase and threatening court action.

Dent contended the purchase of the four Packmaster collection boxes from Island Supply Co. of Grand Island was an "illegal act on the part of City Council and the officers of the city." He cited the failure to advertise for competitive bids, the lack of an ordinance to set up a garbage collection system and the lack of any budget provision for the purchase in the 1950-51 fiscal year.

The council had voted unanimously in favor of the purchase two days earlier, but quickly retreated. McFarland asked Island Supply Co. to return the purchase order.

So it was left to the new mayor and council to implement the garbage collection change the old mayor and council had begun. It was a no-win proposition.

The new garbage ordinance was approved by the council May 22. Mendenhall and the four members elected on the reform slate had taken office April 10.

Residential rates would be $1.10 a month. Garbage and rubbish were to be kept in separate containers of specified sizes. Burning of trash would be allowed only in closed incinerators.
There were other hints of trouble in that council meeting. Horace Crosby was appointed "special counsel for the city in all matters pertaining to validity of past annexation ordinances." Apparently there had been some oversights during previous administrations.

The annexation problem had been brought up at the last council meeting *"when it was learned outlying territory supposedly annexed in 1949 was not officially brought into the city because all state annexation regulations had not been complied with."*

And another of those "little" things invariably guaranteed to irritate some part of the public was mentioned. *"The council turned over to the police committee the task of checking on equipment to become necessary under the city's new dog ordinance, which becomes effective June 1."*

Animal control measures then would be difficult to imagine now. There was no humane society, and facilities for animals were minimal. A letter to the editor May 24 urged:

...the mayor and city council, have passed a new ordinance concerning dogs. I would like to make one suggestion. Clean up the dog pound before collecting stray dogs and placing them in such an environment as we now have. The city has never given a dog catcher enough money or anything else to suitably take care of dogs and the present dog catcher does not have suitable quarters in which to place any dog, thoroughbred or mongrel.

If we claim to be such an up and coming city and improve on this and something else, it's about time the city started with the dog pound.

The present pay for the dog catcher is 25 cents for each pair of ears he takes to the police station proving that he has disposed of a dog after the three day limit. Personally, that is the most disgraceful thing I have ever heard of. If the owner claims his or her dog before the three day limit, the owner is charged for board of the animal. How would you like to kill an animal, then cut his ears off to receive 25 cents?

The mayor and city council should give a man or woman enough money in order to run a decent place and a decent place should be constructed by the city or by a group of local dog lovers or some civic group enabling a man or woman to manage a good dog pound.

And a dog catcher should not be paid according to how many ears he takes to the police station.....

The new council members may have found the process of governing more tedious than exciting.

For example, a May 6, 1952 council meeting as reported in the May 7 Telegraph-Bulletin had the typical list of city issues to consider. A request for a concrete driveway and drain culvert was referred to the city engineer. An application to connect with a city sewer was rejected since it came for a residence outside the city limits. An application to build a duplex on too small a lot was rejected. A complaint about cows being kept on East 13th St. was referred to the Board of Health. A request by Tony Savorelli, manager of Tucker's Cafe, for an ordinance to allow entertainment such as radio, television and musical performances in Class C liquor establishments was referred to committee. *"After a long debate, plans for drainage of Paving District 123 presented by Special Engineer Nosky were approved."*

So it went for a long string of similar issues: traffic problems, paving districts, building codes, a bit of paving in Cody Park. For the councilmen elected to fight crime and vice in 1951, this must have been less fun than they had bargained for. Three of them would decline to seek re-election in 1953.

By 1952, cleaning up the town had a different meaning than it had in 1951. The Retail Committee of the Chamber of Commerce now was asking for cleaner streets.

In a May 9, 1952 editorial, Telegraph-Bulletin editor Cliff Sandahl pressured the council to act on the Retail Committee request:

"....desirous of ridding our streets of a winter's accumulation of dust, dirt, gravel and other forms of grime, the Committee has drawn up a resolution for presentation to the City Council calling for a thorough spring sweeping and washing job."

The mayor declined because, he said, the silt and trash would clog the storm sewers. A compromise plan for a spring sweep down was agreed upon.

City government inevitably irritates citizens in large and small ways. Assistant Police Chief Millard Calhoun announced that beginning April 7, the five-cent fine for overparking in a meter zone would be replaced with a 25 cent fine, and fines would have to be paid at the police station rather than deposited in a *"courtesy envelope."*

In addition to cleaner streets, the Chamber of Commerce also wanted a new truck parking plan in the downtown area allowing easier access for loading and unloading, the newspaper reported on April 2.

Truck traffic on West 12th, still a hot topic half a century later, was an issue that stirred heated discussion at an April 2, 1952 council meeting, the newspaper reported April 3. A five-year-old girl had been killed when she was hit by a truck at 12th and Vine on March 20.

Typical of the irritation that would be caused by any attempt to update dog control activities was a letter to the editor in the Telegraph-Bulletin April 15.

What's the matter with our city officials?

All we have heard since the last election is keep your dogs tied or penned up.

There are a lot more important things to argue about these days.

We need a few ex-service men with families and two or three old maid school teachers to help run things.

We citizens better wake up or we will have to keep our kiddies penned up, too.....

There are more vicious people walking the streets than all the dogs in town. And they don't get tied or penned up.

It really burns me up to think of a $25 fine.....

Whether they wanted to or not, the new mayor and council members were being pushed to take on responsibilities that had previously been neglected or passed on to non-governmental agencies. It was also getting regular lobbying by the Chamber of Commerce.

A special Chamber committee meeting with the Municipal Airport Board on June 4 complained that *"the city had not given its airport sufficient financial support to make possible completion of plans to occupy the new administration building."*

For approximately 30 years prior to 1951 the airport was developed without any appropriation from the city. It was pointed out that, through the years, the port had developed into about a million dollar investment with the city investing considerably less than a hundred thousand dollars.

It was also stated that the port did about $500,000 worth of business per year and sustained a payroll of about $25,000 per month.

The primary source of funds for development have been federal allocations, funds from the state aeronautic board collected on aviation gas tax and revenue from operation.

In the last year the city has collected a one half mill tax levy for airport development. Mayor Mendenhall and councilman Ed Johannesen said the city plans to increase this levy to one mill ....

The municipal airport board has approximately $500 in its treasury. It was shown that his amount is totally inadequate for present needs.

Strong sentiment was expressed to the effect that the airport was a vital asset to the community and was worthy of municipal support that would allow it to develop more rapidly than it can on the basis of using only revenue for development.

The June 28 Telegraph-Bulletin carried a story quoting City Clerk Roy Mehlmann saying *"Operating costs have gone up in all phases of city management"* explaining a $23,200 municipal budget increase.

He attributed the rise in costs to the general rise in prices all over the nation.

The budget passed by the city council was $412,000 compared to the 1951-52 expenditures of $383,000. The tax levy was unchanged at $24.90 per $1,000 of assessed valuation.

Largest increase was for the Municipal Airport, $6,000 for runway maintenance and improvements. The library fund was increased by $5,200.

Reform accomplished, reformers are defeated

The reform group that received overwhelming support from voters in the 1951 city election would be overwhelmingly rejected two years later even though it had been successful in achieving its major goal of eliminating wide-open prostitution and gambling in North Platte

The problem began before Kirk Mendenhall and the reform council members were elected. Mayor Sydney McFarland and his council had decided to make a major change in the garbage collection system. The implementation had been left to Mendenhall and the reform council along with four holdover members from the old council.

As the 1953 election neared, the Telegraph-Bulletin said main campaign issues had been *"garbage collection and vice and crime."* An April 3, 1953 story contained a review of the campaign.

....Two factions lined up for political pot shots. One was headed by Clarence J. Frazier, councilman from the first ward and candidate for mayor, and the other was captained by Mayor Kirk Mendenhall, candidate for re-election. Frazier's group called itself the Civic Improvement Group and Mayor Mendenhall heads the Citizen's Committee, using the same party name that swept him into power two years ago.

Frazier lined up one ex-councilman, T. F. Crawford, to run on his slate for council posts, along with an auto dealer, a real estate man and a railroad conductor.

Mayor Mendenhall lost three of the councilmen who took over the city government with him two years ago. They declined re-election. His slate includes Vern Lyons, present councilman, a service station operator, a Union Pacific ticket agent and a chiropodist.

Two women joined Frazier's slate as school board candidates for two positions opening in May. They are Mrs. Floyd K. Morris and Mrs. Paul Latschar, both active in civic groups and the PTA.

Throughout his campaign, Councilman Frazier has struck at the present garbage collection system, "lack of leadership" in the

police department and the city airport, which he said should pay its own way.

Frazier said that if elected he would attempt to place the police department under civil service to give the department job security for the first time in its history. He said civil service would not necessarily mean an increase in wages.

On the other hand, Mayor Mendenhall has said the garbage system was originally set up on Frazier's recommendations to council and defended the system as the cheapest and most efficient obtainable at this time.

Mayor Mendenhall has defended the police department, calling it the most efficient the city has ever had and directly responsible for cleaning up the former vice and prostitution which existed in North Platte. He added that the city airport has now been placed on a paying basis and is returning large dividends to the city.

Councilman Frazier voiced dissatisfaction with the non-official truck route which passes through the east and north sides of the city and promised to do something for the people of that district if he were elected April 7.

Mayor Mendenhall countered by saying that council was working on the problem and he ordered the street department to treat the streets chemically to hold down dust. He added that he would ask council at is next meeting, April 8, to have a state engineer brought to North Platte to study the truck route problem and offer suggestions for possible solution.

Main speaker for the north side residents involved in the trucking dispute has been Lee Soltow, candidate for council from that ward. He denied that the truck route problem was brought up at this time as a campaign issue but said he was glad it did come up because it tied in with the "do nothing" council headed by Mayor Mendenhall.

In the April 7 election, Frazier won a "sweeping victory ... in an all-time record breaking turnout of voters in a city election," the Telegraph-Bulletin reported April 8.

It also reported "these immediate reactions:

1. Police Chief Charles R. Dick and two other police department men submit resignations.

2. Chief Dick claims that former North Platte gangsters have

3. New mayor restates major campaign issues and pledges reorganization in the city garbage collection program.

Chief Dick and Detective Sam Drummy and Patrolman Jim Hoylman all submitted their resignations to Mayor Mendenhall today effective at once but agreed to stay on in the department until Frazier takes over April 15.

A record 4,815 votes were cast, exceeding the record vote of 1951 by nearly 200 votes. An additional 229 absentee ballots remained to be counted.

Frazier said he looked upon his victory at the polls as a "vote of confidence" from the people of North Platte.

He said he would initiate the three main planks of his platform, lower taxes, city-owned garbage system, and reorganization of departments to economize, as soon as possible.

Elected with Frazier on his Civic Improvement Group slate were: T. F. Crawford, second ward; Marion A. Keys, third ward; Lee Soltow, fourth ward. Ezra Fisher, a service station operator, was the only Citizen's Committee candidate elected. He would represent the first ward. Crawford was one of the council members defeated by the reform campaign in 1951. He was a retired electrical contractor. Keys was a used car dealer, Soltow was a railroad conductor.

The final canvass gave Frazier 2,937 votes to 2,042 for Mendenhall.

John Alexander and Robert B. Watson won school board seats. Police Judge Claude DeLany, and City Clerk L. E. Mehlmann were re--elected without opposition.

Frazier was 47. He had lived all his life in North Platte and came to the mayor's job after four years as councilman from the first ward and 30 years as an employee of the Union Pacific, the Telegraph-Bulletin reported in its April 8 edition.

He had dropped out of school in the seventh grade, starting with the UP as a machinist's apprentice in 1923 to support his mother after his parents were divorced.

He continued his education by attending night school for three years, studying such subjects as mechanical drawing, mathematics, blue prints and general shop practice.

There were signs that the energy and enthusiasm that had powered the reform slate in 1951 had waned with the successful cleanup against prostitution and gambling. Advertising for the Citizens Committee slate in 1953 was largely a replay of the 1951 emphasis on vice cleanup while voters were apparently more interested in garbage pickup, taxation and other more mundane issues.

The three reform council members who had seen all they wanted of long council meetings and public criticism were replaced on the Citizen's Committee slate by Ezra Fisher, first ward; Harry Huston, a Union Pacific ticket agent, second ward; Dr. H. K. Young, a chiropodist, third ward. Grocery store owner Vern Lyons in the fourth ward was the only reform slate councilman elected in 1951 who sought re-election in 1953.

Compared to 1951, the advertising campaigns were modest, but the letters to the editor were frequent and often critical of the Mendenhall administration. In addition to the irritation with the new garbage collection system and fees, letter writers were angered by the new dog ordinance, trucks that stirred dust on East 12th Street, and taxes.

A full-page Citizens Committee ad on the day before the election reproduced a reduced-size version of the 1951 ad talking about prostitution and gambling and said ***"Remember This/It Can Happen Again! These Men Will Continue to Keep North Platte Clean"*** over pictures of Mendenhall and the four Citizens Committee council candidates.

It was far less effective than the Civic Improvement Group's ad emphasizing ***"Better City Management/ for All the People!/ Vote Civic Improvement/ Thrift, Honesty, Efficiency, Farsightedness."***

Apparently, once the vice cleanup was accomplished, there had been nothing to generate the sort of widespread business and community interest in city government a year earlier. The Citizens Committee did not field a slate of candidates in the 1952 city election and there was only one contested race for the four council seats up for election. Incumbent H. L. Reitan easily defeated Bill Owens in that contest for the second ward seat, 958-321. Melvin Elliott, Clarence Frazier and Chester Macomber, all holdovers from the McFarland council, were unopposed for re-election in 1952.

Ezra Fisher was the only Citizen's Committee candidate to win election in 1953, beating Henry George, his Civic Improvement opponent for the first ward seat, 660-491. But George was appointed on April 14, 1953, to fill the other first ward seat left vacant by the election of Frazier as mayor.

The new council also lost no time acting on Lee Soltow's primary complaint. At the April 14 meeting, Soltow moved and Macomber seconded a motion to order all through truck traffic to remain on Highway 30 through the city. The Mendenhall administration's effort to establish a truck route on East 12th, was ended.

The 20th Century
As They Described It

Styles of writing and reporting change over the years. Here are excerpts, some significant some not, in five-year periods from a century of newspapers.

1900 — After "lo these many years" of depending on lanterns, tallow candles and other primitive devices for relieving the gloom of our streets when the moon is not shining, there is a prospect of plenty of light in the near future. For some time, Superintendent Cunningham has been urging the owners of the water plant here to add an electric light plant. Owing largely to the rather strained business relations which existed ….between the city and company, owing to the former having acted in bad faith, the company for a long time turned a deaf ear.

The Semi-Weekly Tribune, January 23.

1905 — Myriads of flags were flying in every direction and the people lined the streets to form an inspiring sight (as President Theodore Roosevelt made a whistle-stop visit in North Platte).

The Independent Era, May 11.

1910 — Geo. D. Dent, Physician and Surgeon, Office over McDonald Bank. Physicians and Surgeons Hospital/A Modern Institution for the treatment of Medical and Surgical Cases. Graduate Nursing. Physician in attendance day or night. Special accommodations for confinement cases. 721-23 North Locust St.

Advertisement in The Semi-Weekly Tribune, June 24.

1915 — There is open gambling in North Platte. Deny it if you care to, make excuses for it if you so desire, bury your head ostrich-like in the sand with the editor of our esteemed contemporary and shout "spasmodic purity" until you are black in the face this fact stands boldly out. There is open gambling in North Platte. Now men and mothers of men! Are you willing for this open gambling to continue all because you are afraid that by speaking the truth you will be "slandering the town?"…..Our streets are filled with scarlet women!

While it is true that a couple of houses of prostitution have been closed, it is also equally true that the inmates of these same houses are still in town and still plying their nefarious trade.

The Evening Telegraph, April 1.

1920 — The first aerial mail planes will land in North Platte Saturday afternoon when two planes carrying mail will make the trip from Omaha to Cheyenne, stopping in North Platte….where oil and gas will be supplied.

The Evening Telegraph, Thursday, August 19.

1925 — Who has Jim married? Is the prevailing question on the streets of North Platte today, after a wire from the west coast …. The news of Mr. Keefe's marriage came as a surprise to most of North Platte, as while Mr. Keefe has always been classed as "the eligible bachelor," he has never been accused of very serious intentions.

The Evening Telegraph, August 17.
(James T. Keefe was Lincoln County attorney.)

1925 — Mrs. Gertie Pouch, proprietress of the Lotus rooming house, Hazel Johnson and Bernice Marshall were arrested yesterday afternoon by city officers after three North Platte youths, two age fourteen years and the third seventeen confessed they had visited and patronized the rooming house, and declared that the women were guilty of conducting a house of ill fame.

The Evening Telegraph, August 12.

1930 — The committee appointed for that purpose has accepted a design for the proposed Indian statue on Sioux Lookout and the county clerk is advertising for its making and erection. The marker will be cut from Bedford stone, the committee finding that marble, granite or bronze would raise the cost very much above the funds available.

The North Platte Telegraph, December 15.

1935 — North Platte plays host monthly to more than 1,400 transients, according to M. R. Bodenstab, chief of the Federal Transient Bureau here…..Under a new ruling, transients will from now on only be given one meal per day instead of the two "handed out" heretofore.

The Daily Bulletin, July 16.

The North Platte "Arch" over Highway 30 at the west edge of the city was a well-known landmark for many decades. It was torn down when the highway was widened.

1940 — Members of the city council last night agreed to sponsor NYA (National Youth Administration) erection of a youth cabin on the northeast corner of Cody park and appropriated a sum "not to exceed $300 for expenses….Lumber for the building will be donated by the NYA and will come from wrecking of three buildings on an abandoned CCC camp at Halsey.

The Daily Bulletin, February 23.

1945 — Another new name was added yesterday to the North Platte canteen Honor Roll when some 55 to 60 workers from the Champion community served and donated. Champion is 110 miles southwest of North Platte.

The DailyBulletin, May 18.

1950 — The city council of North Platte approved a proposal Tuesday to submit to the voters at the April 4th elections a one mill levy, to be used for recreational purposes. The motion was approved after a petition, with 596 names, was submitted to the council. The petition was circulated by the North Platte Recreation Council headed by Ray Young.

Lincoln County Tribune, February 23

1955 — At its regular meeting Tuesday night City Council….passed an ordinance creating a post of full-time paid park commissioner….Councilman Jack Brandon voiced the only opposition, saying he felt $4,000 was too high a salary and the park commissioner would have little to do during the winter.

The Telegraph-Bulletin, April 20.

1960 — North Platte leaders were jubilant today over announcement that the State Game Commission is planning to buy Buffalo Bill Cody's old "Scout's Rest Ranch" northwest of town to be developed as a tourist attraction .... Don Robertson, member of the Commission from North Platte, said if any such buying is done, North Platte will very likely have to pay a good share of it.

The Telegraph-Bulletin, January 29.

1965 — A fund drive to raise money to finance a low-power television translator to bring to North Platte the programs of the CBS network was kicked off today following a meeting of the city council committee in charge of the project ....The CBS programs will come here from KGIN-TV at Grand Island.

The Telegraph-Bulletin, July 3.

1970 — Doubt is reported among state officials whether the Wild West Show arena stadium at North Platte will be completed by June's Nebraskaland Days as originally planned. Stress tests on the unique stadium design did not meet specifications.... The legislature appropriated $280,000 for the stadium at the 1969 session....It will be used for a summer-long re-enactment of Buffalo Bill Cody's famous Wild West Show as well as the week-long Nebraskaland Days celebration each year.

North Platte Telegraph, October 29.

1975 — The North Platte school board will meet at 12:30 p.m. Monday to set the amount of and date for a school bond election. The amount....is expected to be between $9.5 million and $10 million .... Projects to be financed by the bond issue would include a new elementary in southwest North Platte, a new junior high near Centennial Park, alterations and additions to Senior High to include the present Adams Junior High, and additions and alterations to six elementaries .

The Telegraph, August 16

1980 — The Union Pacific Railroad's $40 million westward classification yard will be unveiled this weekend when the Bailey Yard hosts a Family Day for UP employees and their families on Saturday and an open house for the public on Sunday. The new hump yard, which began operations April 15, has been called the most automated railroad classification yard in the world.

North Platte Telegraph, July 19.

1985 — Julie Meusberger, Miss River City, was crowned at the Miss Nebraska Scholarship Pageant Saturday evening at the North Platte High School Little theater.

Sunday Telegraph, June 2,

(This was the first year of the Miss Nebraska Pageant in North Platte.)

1990 — North Platte touts its Nebraskaland Days celebration as a statewide event with something for everyone….But there is one event on the week-long list of entertainment that doesn't belong at this or any other 1990 celebration. That's the Miss Ladycakes Lingerie Auction … Who came up with this raunchy idea? Such an "auction" is per se in bad taste and offensive. It should be removed from the program.

Editorial in the Lincoln Journal, May 9.

1995 — The nation's biggest celebration marking the 50th anniversary of the end of World War II kicked off in North Platte Thursday with a return of a "troop train" and a revival of the famous North Platte Union Pacific Canteen….The train was late, the speaker system wouldn't work, and the line for free sandwiches, hard boiled eggs, cake and cookies was four people wide and half a block long. One veteran was heard to say it seemed a lot like the war years.

North Platte Telegraph, September 1.

1999 — It was a day of thank-yous and pats on the back for those instrumental in getting the North Platte trails system under way. The Centennial Park Trail Section, one of the major segments of the more than 30 miles of trails and designated roadways throughout the city, was officially opened and dedicated Tuesday afternoon.

North Platte Telegraph, October 13.

Bibliography

Sources for the information in this short history include news-paper files on microfilm at the North Platte Public Library and the North Platte Telegraph. Other sources:

Adamson, Archibald R. *North Platte And Its Associations.* North Platte: The Evening Telegraph, 1910.

Bare, Ira L. and W. H. McDonald editors. *An Illustrated History of Lincoln County, Nebraska And Her People.* Chicago and New York: The American Historical Society, 1920.

Hutton, Mary S. An Early History of North Platte, Nebraska. Unpublished master's thesis, University of Nebraska.

The 1920 history by Bare and McDonald is on available at the North Platte Public Library and the Lincoln County Historical Society.

Adamson's 1910 history is also available at the Library.

Readers interested in local history will also be rewarded by:

Beckius, Jim. *North Platte: City Between Two Rivers.* Arcadia Publishing, Chicago, 2002. Part of Jim Beckius's extensive collection of pictures from the town's past.

Coleman, Ruby. *Heritage Lines, The First 10 Years.* Published by Ruby Coleman, printed by Pro Printing & Graphics, North Platte, 1993. A collection of columns on history and genealogy first published in the North Platte Telegraph.

Connor, Jim; Rowley, Charlene; Waldron, Nancy. *North Platte Cemetery Historical Tour.* North Platte, 2001 and earlier editions. Brief but excellent biographies of many notable North Platte residents.

Greene, Bob. *Once Upon A Town: The Miracle of the North Platte Canteen.* Harper Collins Publishers, New York. 2002.

Klein, Maury. *Vol. I, Union Pacific: The Birth of a Railroad 1862-1893* Doubleday & Company, Inc., Garden City, NY, 1987 and *Vol. II, Union Pacific: The Rebirth 1894-1969*. Doubleday. 1990. Excellent history of the railroad with segments about North Platte's beginning and the rise of William F. Jeffers from call boy at North Platte to president of the Union Pacific.

Reisdorf, James J. *North Platte Canteen: An Account of Heartland Hospitality Along the Union Pacific Railroad*. South Platte Press, David City, NE, 1986. Additional printings 1986, 1988, 1993 and 1998. A good, short history of the North Platte area's outstanding home front contribution during World War II.

Russell, Don. *The Lives and Legends of Buffalo Bill*. University of Oklahoma Press, Norman, OK. 1960. This is the authoritative general biography of Cody.

Thornburg, Billie Lee Snyder. *Sandhills Kid in the City 1927-1938*. Old 101 Press, North Platte, NE 2004. A personal memoir with some chapters describing life in North Platte during the 30s.

Yost, Nellie Snyder. *Buffalo Bill: His Family, Friends, Fame, Failures and Fortunes*. The Swallow Press, Inc., Chicago, 1979. Of the many books about William F. Cody, this is the one that gives most detail to his North Platte years. Mrs. Yost also convincingly sorts out some of the myths and conflicting accounts of Cody's life.

Yost, Nellie Snyder. *Evil Obsession: The Annie Cook Story*. Midgard Press, Lincoln, NE, 1991. Written as a novel but based on careful research and interviews. Except for the principle characters, most names have been changed to protect the guilty, but many have been identified by those familiar with the events and people described.